# This book belongs to

_____

This book is dedicated to my children - Mikey, Kobe, and Jojo.

Paperback ISBN: 978-1-63731-715-0
Hardcover ISBN:978-1-63731-717-4
eBook ISBN: 978-1-63731-716-7

Printed and bound in the USA.
NinjaLifeHacks.tv

Ninja Life Hacks®
by Mary Nhin

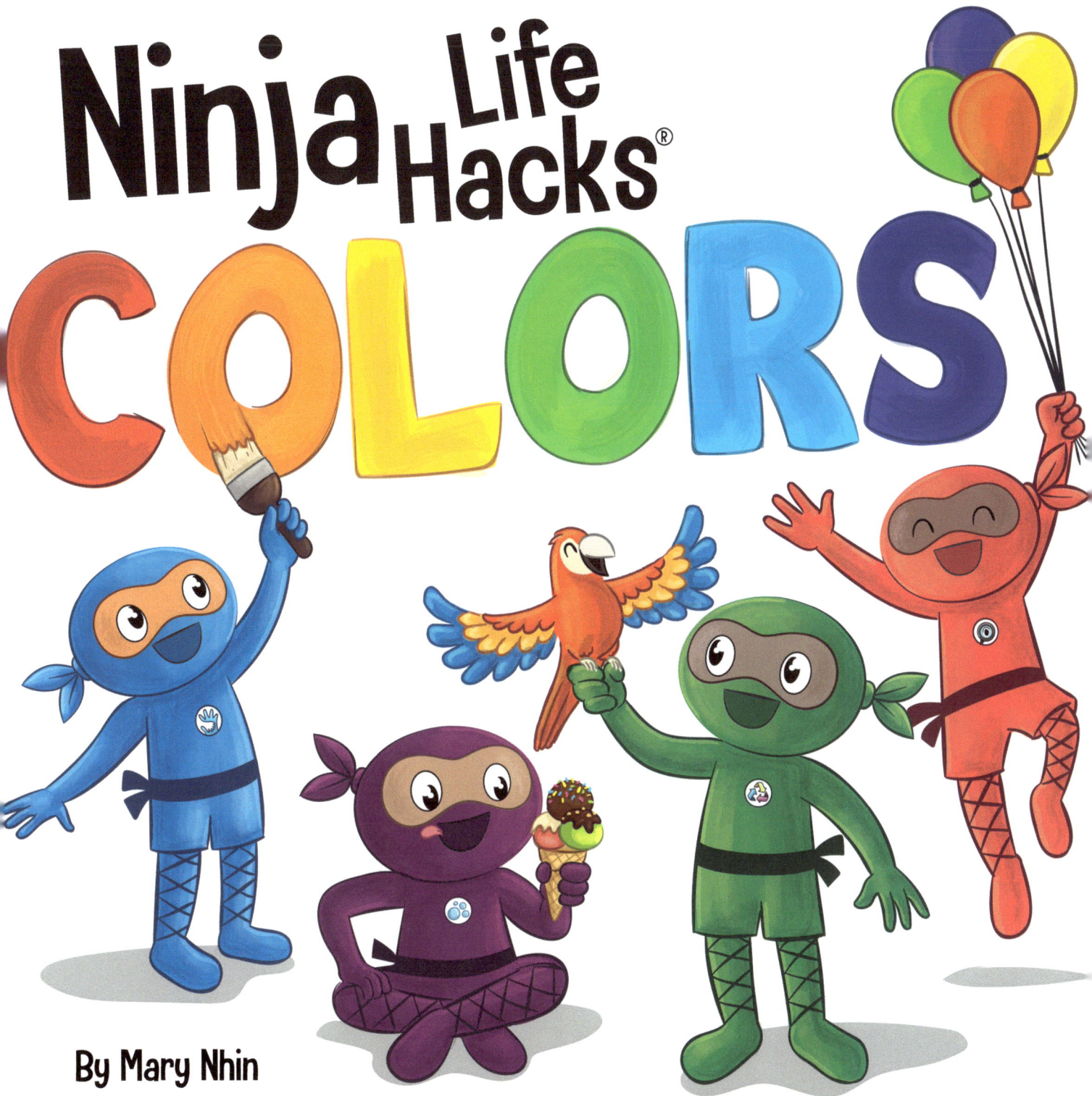

# Ninja Life Hacks
## Life Hacks
# COLORS

By Mary Nhin

A ninja knows all about COLORS
Because ninjas set themselves apart
By always working extra hard
On practicing their colors and art!

**Red** can be a warning sign,
For **focus** and for **love**.

STOP

It can also be for **anger** and **frustration**,
Which ninjas work to rise above.

# Orange is for being **adaptable** and **inclusive**
Like inviting someone to play.

It's also for **gratitude**, so that no matter what,
You'll have an awesome day.

**Yellow** is a bright, warm color—
It's the color of the sun.

A ninja knows when they see yellow,
They're about to have some **fun**!

# Green

is for the leaves, grass, and **earth**,
For all of nature's wealth.

You know what else green can stand for?
**Green** is for **good health**!

**Blue** is for being **helpful** and **patient**,

# Organized and ambitious too.

| WAKE UP | 8:00 |
|---------|------|
| BREAKFAST | 8:30 |
| PHONICS | 9:00 |
| MATH | 10:30 |
| LUNCH | 12:00 |
| SCIENCE | 12:30 |
| CHORES | 14:00 |
| FREE TIME | 16:00 |

But some think of **loneliness** or **sadness**,
When they say they're feeling " blue."

# Purple

is all about **playfulness**,
**Curiosity** and **growth**,

# An **open mind** and **flexible-thinking**

Is where you can learn the most.

Ninjas love that **pink** is for **perfection**

And using **memory** skills each day.

**Pink** can also be for staying **unplugged**
When you want to play!

There are many more COLORS and meanings,
All of which ninjas know!

Which is why when they look up to the sky
A rainbow helps them grow!

Continue the learning with our fun lesson plans which include superpower skills practice, STEM activity, craft, and more! Visit ninjalifehacks.tv

@marynhin  @officialninjalifehacks
#NinjaLifeHacks

Ninja Life Hacks

Mary Nhin    Ninja Life Hacks

@officialninjalifehacks

www.ingramcontent.com/pod-product-compliance
Lightning Source LLC
Chambersburg PA
CBHW042026090426
42811CB00016B/1761